HOLE BY HOLE

A WALK WITH GOD
ON THE GOLF COURSE

DAVID W. COBB

Copyright © 2022
By David W. Cobb

Published by David W. Cobb
Cover Art by: Jeanly Fresh Zamora
Edited by Writing By Michele, LLC, Tulsa, OK

Printed in the United States of America.

ABOUT THE AUTHOR

October 28, 2021

It was on such a day as this that this book was planted in my heart. A day on the golf course filled with clouds and mighty wind, followed by a brilliant sunset. I had been rating golf courses on a panel with *Golfweek Magazine* for some time before finally visiting Prairie Dunes in Hutchinson, Kansas from my hometown of Tulsa, Oklahoma.

The experiences that God was leading me through at that time took me from the selfish world of a bachelor to a man devoted to his wife and a son who, as this book finds its way to print, is about to graduate from high school. When my son was born, my life changed from one of numerous rounds of golf to many hours coaching everything from football to lacrosse. Time seeking God and with my family has been worth every lost round and has given me a life filled with Christ, one that now finds me walking with God on and off the golf course.

My prayer is that this book will bless you and that day by day, moment by moment, hole by hole you find yourself walking with God in all that you do.

Dedicated to Dawson
May you always seek to walk more closely
with your Heavenly Father.

CONTENTS

If you have heard Jesus Christ's voice on the billows, let your convictions go to the winds, let your consistency go to the winds, but maintain your relationship to Him.

—Oswald Chambers

FOREWORD

You identify me in the names of St. Andrews, Pebble Beach, Pinehurst or Augusta, and many of you have experienced my better nature there. But most of you have become acquainted with me in names less well-known, and yet there, to you, I am as familiar as anything you know. For many of you have known me from your youth, and hole by hole I have taught you many lessons. These lessons were not only meant to help you along the links, but also to aid you in your life.

But today, it seems many who I thought knew me the best have not lived out what I sought to teach them. And they have sadly gone the way of the man in the Scriptures who looks at himself in a mirror and then walks away, forgetting what he looks like (James 1:24).

It has been a long time since I have wanted to reach

out to you, and I cannot wait any longer. I may be the only constant place in sport that you will visit until you leave this earthly realm. You cannot conquer me, and so I remain the one last playing field where your competitive fire may still burn. By nature I am vast and ever changing, and in each round you find the consistent challenge you love.

I am the Golf Course, and I know you well better than you might even know yourself.

Outside my grass covered boundaries, there is a troubled world and I fear, for too many of you, I have brought more of that into your lives when that was never my intention. And yet you always seem to return to me, though some decide to find their folly elsewhere. It is my hope that you will come back to me next time carrying a different countenance upon you, and once again be filled with the joy and limitless possibility that you once brought my way when you were young.

Before we go on, I must get something off my chest. I was never intended to be a source of meaning or fulfillment in your lives. So much has been made of me in an attempt to immortalize golf and the players with more skill. Oh, most certainly we have experienced many memorable moments together. Like the time you made that hole-in-one or sank that impossible 40-foot putt. (It was actually 30 feet, but hey, who is counting?)

One of my favorite memories was the time your child hit their first shot that actually made it off the ground. Oh, how you celebrated—tossing them in the air, then dancing about in exuberance. All the pomp from the great tournament competitions and the celebrations that followed can't compare to that moment. I was that place where you found you could connect and strengthen the bond you so desired with your earthly father. For far too many of you, I was the place where you could escape from him and an ever-troubling world.

My favorite times were when you were alone with me, walking in peaceful freedom—not riding in one of those golf carts that so often scar my fairways and landscape. (Golf carts are a definite sore spot with me. Next time you drive one, please do it as gently as possible.) There were also times when you experienced my many challenges without expectation or even keeping score, yet feeling renewed, refreshed and exhausted. Yes, those are the moments I cherished together with you.

Some memories, you might like to forget. Like the time you threw your club and it landed on top of a house, or the time you broke that golf club. (Well, that was not the only club you broke, but again, who is counting?) Or the time you improved your lie under the guise of something called "winter rules" to justify your transgression—which seems, depending upon necessity, to be now part of the rules for so many year-round. And that language you have used following a golfing misfortune would not make your mother proud.

Now, let's talk about a few of your more famous golfers. After all, many of those you most admire both inside my bounds and away from me have been far from perfect. Bobby Jones and Payne Stewart are good examples. Bobby threw his clubs with the best of them and even quit—yes, quit—right in the middle the British Open after carding a less than favorable number on one of my holes there.

As for Payne, well, let's just say for a while golf was all about him. That is, until he found the One whom, without His hand, I would not exist and gave His life back to Him. That is when everything changed for Payne, as it does for all who bring Jesus with them when they visit me. Payne became quite the champion where it truly matters, and also won a few nice golf tournaments. He really held fast to tradition in the way he dressed; some of the fashion a few of you bring with you these days really concerns me.

Now, a little about me... You see, before golf found your ancestors, I was pretty much left alone. Other than walks through my sandy dunes that linked people to the sea, most of my company was kept with rabbits and sheep who worked to keep my turf in excellent condition. But it was along these strolls in those early days that the fancy for golf was born. I was introduced to family and friends, and it was not long until I spread to every corner of the globe.

Why? Well of course, no pun intended, I would like to think it was because of me, but really it was because we found something very special together. A game that was always challenging, exciting, and most of all, fun! You might say I became a metaphor for adventure in life.

I ask you this simple question:

Is golf truly fun today for you, those you play with and those who play around you? Or have I become just a petty diversion, a temporary respite from your troubles and, God forbid, the only adventure in your life? Or just a way for you to focus on something other than your daily grind and misery?

Oh, how I wish you would become like a child again and come back to me with that same freedom you had in those early days. It is never too late to breathe life back into your golf game, just as it never too late to leave the struggles of your life behind and be born again.

When it comes to renewal, you might argue that it is possible for some, but you don't know me. Or you might say, "What does it matter? This game of golf is not my life." But you know in your heart that this game of yours and how you play is but a reflection of your life, and when it comes to golf and life, many of you are just barely breathing.

Let's take a look at one such golfer who is gasping for air as he visits one of my best venues.

Located in the heart of North America is a golf course called Prairie Dunes. The wind breathes across the land there, just as it does where you find me by the sea, and the stronger the wind blows there, the more I come alive. The wind on the true links has the potential to work the same way God does when He gives you the Holy Spirit as a mighty wind that brings peace to your soul and clarity to your walk. Far from distracting and frustrating, the wind on the links can breathe life into those golfers who will yield to it.

Over many years, the land you see at Prairie Dunes yielded to the wind, and it created the best in me—from dramatic, massive sand dunes to subtle, undulating contours flowing like gentle, rolling ocean waves across emerald-green fairways. But for the golfer to fight this wind is futile. Instead, you must continue to yield to the wind, as you do to the Spirit, and in obedience your swing will find freedom.

To Prairie Dunes has come a golfer in need of the Spirit's grace and breath of life. In this golfer, we find the weariness of one who has not only fought futilely against the winds of the links, but also has been worn away by the turbulence of the world. Just about everyone now calls him Bill, but I still call him Billy, because behind this despondent presence I still see that boy who, not long ago, was filled with energy and wide-eyed possibility.

His appearance now looks almost as if he has spent too many lonely, blustery days visiting rough places less like the links and more like a forest. Where the wind becomes an annoying distraction as the churning autumn leaves of his life went this way and that. Unlike one blessed with the gift of the Holy Spirit, he seems beaten down by more of what the world has offered in the way of futility and striving.

This loss of heart we see can only be overcome by moving forward with God, and fortunately for even those like Billy, this newness of life is closer than one might think. It is on Prairie Dunes with me where an unexpected rendezvous with hope awaits Billy.

Let's look on together to see if he may find a better way here with me on the golf course today.

TRANSFORMATION

THE REASON FOR
PLAYING THE COURSE

What happens when you die? Of course, this is the most important question we all face. This question is answered by your response to another question. What happens to a man while he lives? He chooses a path, and the chosen path answers the question.

Have you answered that question? You are doing it right now...moment by moment, day by day, or if you are a golfer, hole by hole.

You must lose everything if you want to have everything.

It is one thing to walk the course by yourself and another to sadly walk the course alone. Our story's golfer, Billy Newman, used to believe it was easier to walk the course alone. Now, he is finding that what seemed hard before could be the easiest way to find restoration.

FAITH

THE FIRST HOLE

For it is by grace you have been saved, through faith—
and this is not from yourselves, it is a gift from God.
— Ephesians 2:8

When it comes to renewal, it might be argued by most that regardless of circumstance there is always hope—that is, unless you are the one experiencing despair. When it comes to golf and life, Billy Newman is just barely breathing.

Billy normally feels in control, but lately his life is out of control and the very mechanisms that have brought him some peace now torment him all the time. What can he do? How did he now find himself in this predicament?

"How ironic it is that I have traveled the world, and this is the last one," Billy Newman tells himself. *This* would be the last of the top 100 golf courses he has yet to play. The golf course, Prairie Dunes, is located in southern Kansas, not far from Billy's home state of Oklahoma, but forever away from just about anywhere else.

From Pebble Beach to St. Andrews, Billy has seen the great golf courses by living a life most golfers dream of, reviewing and writing about these destinations. He has played golf in places where the beauty is beyond belief— from holes winding through the lushness of Eden to the barren wastelands of the desert, from holes driving through the rainforest to those slung on the sides of cliffs, above the ocean, presenting views that only golf would provide to those golfers who would dare venture to the ends of the earth.

As he looks out at the course he is about to play, Billy tells himself, "This is it. After today, I will have seen them all."

Not bad for someone who is barely forty years old. It is quite an accomplishment. But Billy doesn't see it that way.

The problem with Billy is that he is far from content with his life. In fact, he is downright miserable and has been that way for quite some time. And it seems that even a golf course, which used to provide some refuge to his suffering, has now become a part of his misery.

Even a golf course like Prairie Dunes. For that is where he was heading a few days ago when he first learned some news that still bothers him. As he drove, he could not force it out of his mind. One of his high school classmates had died. He received this message in an email sent to his entire high school class. The title of the email was Sad News.

The body of the email read as follows.

It is with sad news that I must tell you all that Adam Brooks has passed away.

Adam was very successful with investments and the stock market. He died driving his Porsche Carrera GT on the racetrack.

He leaves behind a wife and a son.

What perplexed Billy was the fact that this news ate at him, especially since he had not been close friends with Adam since, well, since… And with this reminiscing, Billy pushed back a painful memory and redirected his attention to the road ahead. But just as quickly as the tumbleweeds raced across the road, his thoughts once again found their way back to Adam.

Billy had not seen Adam since they graduated from high school twenty years ago. And yet he could still picture Adam's youthful, ruddy face. He could also recall how Adam loved cars. Billy thought to himself, "What was that old car that Adam used to be so proud of and used to covet so deeply? Was it a '75 Oldsmobile or Camaro?"

Billy's mind then drifted back to high school, since his twenty-year class reunion was just around the corner, and he smiled as he thought about seeing his fellow classmates again.

Then Billy found himself thinking about Adam again. "At least he died doing something he loved," he thought to himself. But he could not shake the last sentence in the email about how Adam had left behind a wife and a son. In that instant, the image of Billy's own son blazed in his mind, making him smile, giving him a warm feeling of joy mingled with melancholy.

How could Billy be anything but joyful? After all, it had been ten years since he set his mind on a definite, major purpose. Goal after goal he had accomplished, until now he reached both financial and critical success amongst his peers, in his community, throughout the nation and even internationally.

It had also been ten years since his son was born. Billy was a success, wasn't he?

The trouble with Billy is that he does not feel like a success. Apart from the successful appearance that Billy exudes, on the inside he feels afraid of being found out as the fraud he truly deep in his heart believes he is. One would never have known this to be true, as Billy is a master poseur, hiding behind story after story of his most interesting exploits. All the while, he is scared to death of the truth—that he believes he is a failure and could never live up to the expectations he thinks he must achieve. One day, he fears, his successful facade will be taken away, and the real person he is inside will be revealed.

Billy's fear drives all that he does. And to be fair, he often reasons he has a right to protect himself. After all, he has striven and given everything to achieve his personal success, and he would do anything to preserve what he has earned.

And there is no other area of his life that tells the story of this tenacious competitive fire that burns inside him like sports. Whether it is football, basketball, baseball, golf or any number of other sports he has played since his youth, with each one Billy cannot help but take the field to prove himself, really to prove his worth. His first love was football, and he still occasionally recollects his prowess on the gridiron while he was in high school. It was this early love of football where he first learned that sports could be an outlet, really a vehicle, to send a message to others that despite his insecurity, he indeed has what it takes to be a success.

This youthful love of football really was not Billy's first true love, for that was reserved for a girl named Megan. And as he drove down the road a few days ago, Billy's thoughts turned to her.

It is at this one moment that Billy's thoughts now return to the present as he has arrived at his destination.

Located in the heart of North America is Prairie Dunes. The wind breathes across the land there, just as it does by the seaside links, and the stronger the wind blows here, the more the game of golf comes alive. The wind on an authentic, true links golf course has the potential to work the same way God does when He gives you the Holy Spirit as a mighty wind that brings peace to your soul and clarity to your walk. Far from distracting and frustrating, the wind on the links can breathe life into those golfers who will yield to it.

Over many years, the land you see at Prairie Dunes has yielded to the wind, which has created dramatic, massive sand dunes combined with subtle, undulating contours that flow like a gently rolling ocean across emerald-green fairways. Billy knows it is futile for a golfer to fight the wind when it is gusting across the links, and today it looks like there is not much fight left in him.

Every time Billy has played golf, somewhere along the way during his round he has found the fresh air of freedom he once experienced in his life. Like a drug, the

24

golf course has become the only place he has found to leave the weariness of his futile fight against turbulent winds of this world—winds he so willingly yielded to so many years ago. He is usually too wrapped up in seeing one more golf course to realize that it is the solitude that has provided his relief.

In Billy, there are traces of that boy who not long ago was filled with energy and wide-eyed possibility.

We also find in Billy the discouraging presence of one who seems less than enthusiastic about being on the course today. He might just walk away. In truth, he thinks about doing that the minute he steps out of the car and feels the cold autumn winds, which he knows must be clipping along at up to 30 miles per hour. He does not waste any time warming up before heading to the first tee.

His clubs are strapped on his back, and each step he takes is laborious, with a noticeable limp that has been nagging him for some time. As he makes his way with his head down, he more closely resembles one trudging off to hard labor than a golfer doing what he loves. It has been quite a while since he has brought any passion with him to this game, and he does not feel today will be the long-awaited day his fire returns and he stops just going through the motions. He tees up his ball and is on his way down the first fairway.

The winter rye in the fairway is a striking green in contrast to the waning fall landscape, and Billy's eyes change from blue to grey, reflecting this late October day. The first hole sharply bends to the left, and as he turns to address his ball, the stiff wind that aided him down the fairway now presses relentlessly against his back so much that he can barely keep his balance. He can see the flag stick in the distance, with the dune to the left that concealed it from the tee now protruding out just enough to taunt him. To the right, a small stream beckons the ball hit with even the slightest fade.

Billy sets up, laboring to maintain his balance in the gale and swings, although it is really more of a chopping motion that sends his ball aimlessly airborne. Quickly, the wind takes control, mercilessly sending his ball to rest into the riparian golf ball graveyard to the right.

Billy knows the hard truth. His ball is gone. However, even with this knowledge, just as always, it never keeps him from looking for lost balls no matter how unlikely it is he will find them. It is as if he finds the same value in the golf ball as the shepherd who would leave the ninety-nine to find the one lost sheep.

But he cannot find this ball, and after a few minutes of looking, he drops another. His hope arises anew with a crisply hit shot that lands softly on the lowly slung green. After two putts, he is ready to move on.

It's not the way most golfers would like to begin their day, but not a complete disaster either, and Billy seems relieved. He pauses for a moment in the calm provided by the dunes that protect this hollow. His deeply furrowed brow softens, and I see a gleam of hope in his eyes.

HOPE

THE SECOND HOLE

*Who hopes for what they already have? But if we hope
for what we do not yet have, we wait for it patiently.*
                                                —Romans 8:24–25

There is something about Prairie Dunes that causes Billy
to reflect back to his childhood. He begins to recall events
he has not thought of in many years. He smiles as he recalls
breaking into his father's liquor cabinet and taking a bottle
of his Jack Daniels to the golf course where he had his first
drink with friends while playing golf.

He then pushes away any thoughts of what alcohol has
done to his life, or of his other present sufferings away from
the golf course. He is being thrust backward to that simple
time of childhood, much of which was spent playing on
a golf course designed by Perry Maxwell. It is perhaps the
memory of those days that draws him back to a happier
time.

I am not here to reflect or become lost in nostalgia. I am here to rate this course, he thinks to himself. This is work that Billy has done for almost ten years, and he now refocuses to do it once more. Even though he knows Prairie Dunes does not need his stamp of approval, as the course has been perpetually lauded as one of the best courses on the planet, he sees it as his duty to uncover aspects of the course that others may have missed.

It is this self-importance, really this pride, that now motivates him to schedule a round of golf. He hides this from himself with a well-rehearsed air of false humility. Billy is a master when it comes to self-deception because in reality, the only thing he now cares about is his golf score.

Billy knows Perry Maxwell's courses well and admires his other designs, places like Southern Hills, Crystal Downs and Colonial. He has always enjoyed the way Maxwell would thoughtfully use the existing lay of the land to guide the steps golfers would walk, and he is already quite impressed with Prairie Dunes. He can already see how, by patiently surveying how the land takes shape, a designer like Maxwell can bring to life a golf course that moves players down the path they naturally would stroll along, whether there were golf holes present or not. And even with all of his self-important posing, Billy finds it difficult to not just let go and enjoy what many consider to be Perry Maxwell's greatest masterpiece.

Billy cannot, however, let go.

As Billy surveys the second hole, he feels that all too familiar confusion and hesitancy, or loss of heart, come over him. It is a shallow feeling of despair that beckons to him and tells him that when it counts, he really doesn't have what it takes to make it.

The second hole is a par 3 that measures 161 yards. The green is elevated and tucked into the base of a thirty-foot high sand dune with five bunkers surrounding it. The bunker most golfers find is twelve feet deep and fronts the center of the green. The dune, which continues to climb to the right, is covered in tall grass and plum thicket. It is a beautiful sight, pleasing to the eye, but when it comes time to strike the ball, his reaction is one of cautious anxiety.

Billy's heart is pounding violently as he addresses the ball. He fidgets, and the hope in his face has turned into concern. He steps away from the ball and then sets up again, his club repetitively waggling behind the ball. Finally he relents and swings, but his follow-through lacks commitment and his ball, while traveling straight toward the green, comes up woefully short.

Billy believes the next shot will be critical to the final results of his round today. Will Billy give into resignation and just go through the motions or anxiously tense up due to recent failure? Or will he find what he cannot perhaps even remember in the midst of the battle, that swing of his past that has so many times sustained him? He summons what has carried him so many times before—the will to keep his despair in check and his game from falling apart.

He searches for a memory of past success. The first time he played The Old Course at St. Andrews comes to mind. Yes, he is seeking the same swing that helped him par the first hole there, a swing that softly placed his approach safely over the Swilkan Birn, leaving him just inches from the hole.

Billy knows he must find that better part of his game here because his ball rests at the bottom of the deep swale. He must climb the steep slope to even see the flag stick, which is positioned directly behind the cavernous bunker. His next shot finds that better memory, and with it, the commitment that he first had lacked. He runs up the bank to find his ball just a few feet from the hole.

Now, hope has turned into anticipation of even better golf to come.

LOVE

THE THIRD HOLE

*And now these three remain faith, hope and
love: but the greatest of these is Love.*
—1 Corinthians 13:13

At Prairie Dunes, the third tee box is perched upon a
massive sand dune that borders the left side of the hole all
the way to the green. When Billy stands on this tee box,
he views before him a sea of grass with a thin ribbon of
fairway in the distance below and to his right, looking
much the same as the Colorado River might appear to
someone standing on the rim of the Grand Canyon.

It is here our golfer really experiences the true measure
of wind, not gusting but constantly, relentlessly flowing.
To complicate matters, the wind is not coming completely
from behind but instead is pressing down on him from
right to left, so that any hint of a pull or a hook will lead
to disaster.

Billy attempts to gather himself for a practice swing and loses his balance, but instead of feeling despair, he laughs. He pulls his left arm across his body and smiles with a painful grimace, trying to stretch out the shoulder that has bothered him and continued to worsen over the years. He knows that on this golfing precipice, he is about to find either greatness or disaster.

Without hesitation, he steadies himself and swings. There is no lunging or even any effort on his part. The club just rises over his shoulder and swings smoothly down, up, and over to the other. The result is that of harmony and beauty as the ball seeks out the voice of the wind that now has become its best friend. He cannot see where or whether the ball has found the fairway, but in his eyes, there is look of peaceful satisfaction, the gaze of one who in his heart knows the truth.

It had been a long while since Billy has experienced that kind of freedom in a golf shot, and it is this hope that will carry him through the rest of this day. To his delight, Billy does find his ball in the fairway. His next shot sails over the green, and he scrambles to save his par.

Billy can feel success is within his grasp, so with all his will, he is going to reach out to seize it.

For a moment, the shadow hanging over him has been wiped away, and Billy feels the boy in him struggling to hang on to the satisfaction of the moment. But as he steps to the fourth tee, writing down his score and studying the yardage of this par 3, he has the serious look of someone striving to conquer again.

A Good Death

BROKEN

THE FOURTH AND FIFTH HOLES

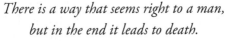

There is a way that seems right to a man,
but in the end it leads to death.
—Proverbs 14:12

When a man builds himself up to be his own god and everything he serves revolves around his own self-made kingdom, in his mind he is very secure, but his heart knows otherwise. Filled with fear that he will lose what he has built, he begins to protect himself in the very ways that will lead to his ultimate destruction.

As Billy stands on the fourth tee box, he surveys the dune that travels the distance of the third hole and continues to make its way north. This is where our man finds the fourth green. The right side of the rather long putting surface is positioned on top of the dune, tilting slightly downhill to the left toward the first of three bunkers that come into play here. The largest of these

33

bunkers dominates the right half of the green, and a small pot-size bunker falls in line behind it, leaving a significant window of opportunity to the left.

This day, the flag is tucked behind the right bunker like the dangling of a carrot. Billy cannot resist aiming for the flag, but instead, his shot finds the bunker from which he can barely blast his ball onto the green. As the ball slowly trickles its way through the blast zone, he hangs his head. Three putts later, and Billy is on his way to the fifth hole, feeling more determined to hang on to this round than ever.

When did Billy begin striving instead of playing golf, exchanging his smooth swing with all of its freedom for one heavily yoked and burden bearing? His next swing is sure to be filled with great effort, but each increasing notch of intensity seems to always be followed by less than desirable results.

Billy makes his way to the long par-4 fifth hole, which turns back to the south, uphill into the teeth of the wind. Billy wastes no time here. He grips his driver so hard, the veins in his forearms almost pop out of his skin. He swings with what must be all his might, snap-hooking his ball into the knee-high grass to the left.

Billy is relieved to find his ball. However, he is only able to will the ball just back into the fairway on his next shot.

Billy is haunted now by the same anxiety that has led him in his life to escape to golf course after golf course. He feels it is just him against the course, for it has now become his enemy. He chunks his next two shots and finally flies his approach twenty feet past the hole. He knows he is not in the right frame of mind to successfully attempt the treacherous downhill putt he faces, which requires surgeon-like precision, and his attempt roars past the hole and off the green. Three heartless shots later, his misery comes to an end along with any hope of salvaging his round.

Now Billy feels rage grip him, and he rips up his scorecard and throws it away.

Why has Billy always felt like he had to strive? From where did this anxiety—really, this loss of heart—come from?

It has been a while since Billy has thought about his dad. Billy's relationship with his father has always been a struggle. For as much as he has tried, he never feels like he measures up to his father's expectations. Billy never feels like he has what it takes to win his father's approval.

Billy tries to push the thought of his father out of his mind, but his dad is always there, impacting everything he does. At the end of every endeavor, this relationship with a man he feels like he can never please, even after all these years, keeps Billy striving to measure up to unrealistic expectations that have driven him into anxiety and even depression. Billy loves the man who is his father, but can never understand his dad and most of all their distant, half-hearted relationship. Why is it so difficult to talk to his father? To feel the love and approval he has longed for all his life?

Tears now race down Billy's cheeks as he thinks about his dad, and he falls to his knees. "God," he prays, "help me understand my relationship with my father." He remains there on his knees for quite some time, yearning for an answer. As he prays, a peace comes over him. He keeps pleading with God.

"Help me understand."

In that moment, Billy hears these words speaking into his consciousness" "What you need to do is ask every man you meet how you can pray for them." This statement fills Billy with both excitement and fear. He knows that this voice is not coming from himself, for it is asking him to do something completely uncomfortable.

Pray for someone else? Billy thinks to himself. *I can barely pray for myself, much less pray for someone else.* But Billy is put at ease by the fact he's all alone on the course, and the prospect of following through with this instruction on a day with such fierce weather as this is unlikely. In fact, Billy has not even seen another golfer since he arrived.

He rises from his knees, but he still feels unsettled. While realizing the great need for reconciling his feelings for his father, Billy does not fully comprehend how deeply his relationship with his father has shaped his life.

Billy thinks back to his childhood and remembers the day everything changed for him. It was the day he found out the truth and began believing a lie. Billy was ten years old when his parents told him he was adopted. From then on, not only has Billy felt like he couldn't measure up; he also believes he doesn't belong and he doesn't have what it takes to be a man. This belief was reinforced by bullying and betrayal by his friends in school. All this did was persuade him to create the perfect mask persona that has made it appear Billy has it all together, when in reality he was and still is self-conscious and insecure.

Billy closes his eyes and thinks back to his first love. Her face would always indelibly be seared into the deep places of his heart. For with Megan, Billy found the thrill of infatuation and desire. With Megan also, he found the terrible pain of deceit and betrayal. She was not only his first love, but also his first loss of innocence. He pushes away the memory, yet the fruit of what happened has impacted his life.

This betrayal, this deep pain, became a favor Billy would repay to others through the years. Insulating himself from feeling deeply, wearing the mask of security, becoming what he once despised and hated, he has hidden his wounds, yet they have still dominated his life. The realization of just how broken he is now comes to the surface, and all the years of pain are flowing like a great whirlwind inside him.

Completely broken and emptied and entering his deepest wounds, Billy now looks like a man who might just be ready to play some real golf. Leaving his scorecard behind and letting go of so much pain, Billy now makes his way to the next hole.

FREEDOM

THE SIXTH HOLE

And he said: "I tell you the truth, unless you change and become like little children, you will never enter the kingdom of heaven."
—Matthew 18:3

Billy has been to some places that have imparted much beauty, but nothing like what he is experiencing while he stands on the sixth tee has ever happened to him. He is suddenly and completely left without any thought of his life as it is, and he is breaking through to just be in the moment. He does not ponder the irony that brokenness can be more than game-changing; it can be life-altering. The inspirational natural beauty and strategy at Prairie Dunes' sixth hole is turning out to be just what Billy needs to dismantle his constructed consciousness and find his heart again.

As Billy stands there soaking it all in, a hope fills him

that maybe he can change. In spite of the carnage that his selfish existence, in all of its brokenness, has left behind, just maybe he can change.

The damage he has inflicted on his family has been especially painful. In his pursuit to be a winner in the world, Billy knows in his heart he is very close to losing his family. Billy closes his eyes, and he can see his children and their innocent, precious faces. He can also picture his beautiful wife. How did they ever drift so far apart?

In the past, he has justified the neglect of his family as the need to provide and to seek his dream. Now, Billy is seeing clearly the lie that he has bought into, and this resolve rises up deep inside him, mingled with regret and a hope of better days to come.

The sixth hole's elevated tee sharply falls downward into the tall wild grass that borders the hole's corridor. Billy wants to remain in this place of freedom and always hold the scene before him. So, he continues to linger here, looking to his left and down upon the second green and then beyond, where he can catch just a glimpse of the first hole where he began his journey. He soaks in the vast, tawny sea of waving grass and deep red plum thickets with trees clinging to the last of their golden leaves.

From here, he can see the sixth fairway gently flowing from right to left like an emerald river that narrows as it reaches the green. The fairway splits two bunkers in the area where most drives would land before skirting another bunker that appears to front the putting surface. To him, there seems to be no mystery to the path to success, but this hole has made many golfers look foolish.

Filled with a new sense of purpose, Billy fires his next drive, a bullet that pierces the wind. On the way to his ball, a light rain begins to fall, flecking his face and mingling with tears. He is having a pleasant conversation with himself, and his recent bitter, angry, self-defeating outburst is now a distant memory.

Can it be? Now, there is joy streaming from his face and a man who just a moment ago was broken, with all of his own expectation drained away, is positioned to freely go about living—or for that matter, playing golf. He has stopped worrying about results on the golf course and simply begins to enjoy himself.

Can it be that he is returning to a time when everything about golf is joyful? When it does not matter how Billy played! Every topped shot, worm burner, shank, hook or slice, every ball that finds any number of hazards, from sand to water to the many balls that end up outside my bounds, or deep down in waist-high grass or far into a forest... Perhaps it doesn't matter, because with every shot, good or bad, there is opportunity and expectation gleaming in his eyes.

It will not take long to put these perceived changes in Billy to the test. Prairie Dune's sixth hole plays to the east, which means the wind is now blowing from Billy's right. He hits his drive with a slight draw that, without any wind, would have placed his ball perfectly in the fairway, just to the right of the fairway bunker on the left. But the wind holds its own, and by the time Billy's ball hits the ground, it has turned helplessly to the left. Once it hits the area just to the left of the fairway, it shoots into the tall grass.

Billy must now carry both bunkers to reach the putting surface. The deep grass rises nearly to his knees, and he wisely blasts out with his ball, carrying the first bunker and rolling just short of the next bunker. From the tee, this bunker looks like it is next to the green, but actually there is some twenty feet between this bunker and the green. This depth perception issue has caused many golfers to come up short on their approach, leaving them a tricky approach through a swale to the green.

Billy must walk around the large bunker to see what faces him. Once he is back to his ball, he must feel his way through this shot. Instead of lobbing the ball at the target, he clips a low, hard, biting shot through the wind. His ball violently bumps the green and propels itself forward, skipping once, then suddenly coming to a halt just a few feet from the hole. Billy sprints around the bunker to see the results, just like he did when he was a boy.

A boy who knew he had what it takes, and now a man who believes that confidence in the future might just be possible again.

BLESSED

THE SEVENTH HOLE

"This is my Son, whom I love; with him I am well pleased."
—Matthew 3:15

The seventh hole's prevailing south wind offers the golfer a welcome respite, but with it blowing at the golfer's back, Billy requires wisdom to match this par five's risk-reward design.

A calm presence or peacefulness has settled over Billy, one very much like that of the humble gratitude of the prodigal son returning home to his Father.

Billy can see that a reasonably well-struck drive riding this wind will produce more than enough distance off the tee. The thought leaves him with the irresistible temptation to go for the green in two, where the risk rarely finds its reward.

As Billy steps to the ball, he hears a voice from behind him say in a deep soft tone, "Do you mind if I join you?" Billy turns around and finds a tall, darkly clad, silver-haired man smiling with a sincere, compassionate gleam in his piercing blue eyes.

Normally, Billy would not want companionship on the golf course, but there is something about this man that makes him oblige. The two men shake hands, and the stranger introduces himself as Bruce. Without any small talk, the golfers are on their way together.

Billy's drive is well struck, riding the wind, leaving him with little more than a mid-iron to reach the green. Lost in his thoughts, he straps his bag over his shoulder and begins to walk down the fairway when he hears the same internal voice that spoke to him on the fifth green. It is not an audible voice as much as it is a whisper within him that says, "I will take your heart of stone and give you a new heart."

Joy leaps within Billy. A new heart and a new start! Can he really be hearing God's voice? Would God care enough to speak to him? As he walks down the fairway, there is a new spring in his step with the wind at his back and God by his side.

When it comes to Billy's relationship to God, much of it has been shaped by his church. In the church, Billy was exposed to the Scriptures, tradition and reason. But now, is God revealing to Billy that he can actually experience God and have a personal relationship with him? Will Billy come to the realization that he no longer has to see God as just somewhere out there in the ether, in Heaven, far away? To Billy, God is so great he can't see how this master of the universe would care about such an undeserving person as himself.

The meaning of *spirit* when translated from Hebrew to English is *wind*. And just as Billy has struggled to master the invisible character of the wind, he has been being perplexed by the same nature of the Spirit working in his life. The Spirit is as powerful and as real as the wind that propels Billy toward the green in the distance. It is the same Spirit that lifts up all men who will yield to its strength, so that God may become perfected in their human weakness.

As Billy arrives to the place where his drive has settled in the fairway, the anxiety and pain are giving way to only the moment and what is coming next in this adventure. Billy will need to stay in the moment during his next shot.

This is where Maxwell's keen understanding of the golfer's psyche now presents Billy with an option that is certain to have left many golfers leaving this hole scratching their heads. The slightly elevated green sits deceptively inviting between two shallow, flat bunkers. The bunker on the left is cut extremely close to the small putting surface. And the opposite bunker, while not hugging the green as closely, is visually more menacing due to the large dune looming above it. This provides a less than imposing look from where Billy now finds himself, one that lures many golfers into a second shot that finds the impossibly dense vegetation on the outside of the bunkers leaving them, if they should even find their ball, helpless to advance it.

Faced with this type of decision, the old Billy would not have hesitated in going for the green, but this new Billy takes the road less traveled and chooses the strategic route. This wise move leads to a satisfying par on a hole where many dreaming of glory are left limping away to the challenging eighth hole in demoralizing defeat.

Bruce calmly follows suit with his par and congratulates Billy on his par, and Billy returns the favor. Unlike most golfing strangers he is forced to play with, Bruce somehow puts Billy at ease. And while intrigued by Bruce, as usual Billy is mostly too consumed with himself to think much more about it. Feeling blessed with his new heart and the revelation of possibly hearing God's voice, he follows Bruce to the next hole.

GRACE

THE EIGHTH HOLE

*I press on toward the goal to win the prize for which
God has called me heavenward in Christ Jesus.*
—Philippians 3:1

Billy is now looking forward to the dramatic sense of
adventure that reaches in and challenges you, testing
whether you have what it takes to succeed. He knows
the 430-yard, par-4 eighth hole, or The Dunes as it is
affectionately named, is one of the great golf holes that calls
out for the best in a golfer.

Billy is now one man, with one hole, one swing, one
step, one life to live, done within the moment. He is not
thinking about anything more than the glory of the present
that is placed before him. If he is to take on the challenge
of a hole like number eight at Prairie Dunes, he knows he
can't be caught in the middle of his next shot, looking to
the past or focusing on the future. He must stay confidently

in the moment.

There is so much uncertainty placed upon the golfer who plays the eighth hole. All the usual suspects are found here—unpredictable bounces; uneven lies; impossibly tall, thick native grass; deep green side bunkers; a severely rolling putting surface; and the wind, oh the wind! These ingredients all come into play perfectly as the eighth hole climbs precipitously upward from tee to green and, like attempting the summit of Mt. Everest, taking the life out of many who have attempted to conquer The Dunes.

The journey for Billy up through The Dunes is daunting, but he looks ready to meet the adventure at hand. His challenge begins with the most demanding drive on the course. The fairway rises in rolling waves into the west before dipping and turning to Billy's right as it disappears behind a sprawling tract of native grass After making this roughly 45-degree turn to the northwest, the fairway climbs again as it makes its way to the green, which is barely visible in the distance. The 30 miles per hour wind from the south makes the already difficult tee shot treacherous.

For the right-handed golfer like Billy, the pressure of a left to right crosswind of this magnitude has brought even the best athletes to their knees. Billy does not seem to be in any hurry to go on his way, but he also does not appear to be procrastinating or frozen in fear. No, he is soaking in everything before him in a very deliberate fashion, like one paying respect to greatness experienced in a moment that may not come again and that will stay in their heart forever.

But now his lingering is at an end, and he struggles

to hold his balance as he stands over his ball, his clothes sticking to his back and flapping furiously in front of him. He swings smoothly, but the ball is caught up in the wind and fading to the right where it mercifully comes up just short of the tall grass.

Bruce steps to the tee and without hesitation fires a long, low drive toward the left center of the fairway. The wind adds just the slightest fade to the ball, and it skips down the fairway, coming to rest with the ideal angle to approach the green.

Billy has left himself a long, blind approach shot that must carry across a large measure of waving grass to reach the green. This is the worst angle from which to approach the green, bringing all three bunkers and the yucca plants that stand guard around them directly into play. His ball is also now below his feet, halfway hidden, settled all the way down in the shallow first cut of rough and resting on the hard pan below. He steadies his balance again, almost as if he is leaning against the gale, and fires a low, driving shot that easily clears the grassy margin on the other side. The ball bolts forward up the slope before losing its momentum, as grace would have it, once again just short of the wheat-high grass, only a few feet from the green.

Billy is looking for his ball on the other side in the valley below, walking up and down the edge of the tall grass opposite from where his ball now lies. He does not believe the ball made it over the grassy hazard. Negativity is a hard habit to break. Why not choose optimism first? Our habits are indeed difficult to change. Billy has been enlightened up to this point today. Now, he needs to be enabled to change the way he thinks.

In golf and in life, we often don't receive what we deserve, but if you've lived long enough, you usually expect the worst. In life it's difficult to give grace to others, or to accept it yourself. But when you receive it during a round of golf, you'll gladly accept it.

After Billy walks up and down the valley a few more times, he shakes his head side to side like the golfer who is certain that his ball is not coming back to him. He straps his clubs over his shoulders and climbs up to the green. For the first time, the sun comes out, casting a golden spotlight on Prairie Dunes, and Billy finds the ball he thought for sure was lost.

Billy smiles and then begins to laugh like someone who has just been given a great gift. A delicate chip shot remains, and Billy executes it flawlessly, before missing his par putt. Bruce rolls in his par, and then the two golfers stop and fondly look back over the hole.

Bathed in the fresh sunlight, the churning grass that Billy had overcome to reach the green looks to him like a living, golden shoreline along the margins of the fairway. He now can see how much more the grass recedes after it crests the hill on the way to the green. Billy's obstacle was much less than he originally believed, but he could only see that by looking back. Now he is really stirring, and his passion is burning within him. As he prepares to leave the mountaintop to embrace with adventure the final hole of the front nine, he suddenly remembers the instruction from the voice he heard earlier.

Billy uncomfortably clears his voice and says, "Is there

anything on your mind that I can help you with or pray with you about?"

The constant smile on Bruce's face grows wider, and he looks back over the dunes and says, "The view from this green always reminds me of just how far I've come and how much grace has been given me." Bruce reaches in his pocket and pulls out a large coin. He flips it in the air and says "Yes, Bill, we so often just don't realize how far we've come and how much grace has been given us and how fortunate we are to be alive. If it wasn't for this coin, I wouldn't be standing here today. This coin was in my grandfather's chest pocket during World War I and stopped a bullet that should have claimed his life."

Billy, who does not realize he has become quite cynical over the years, thinks to himself, *What does this story have to do with me?* He smiles wryly. This is what he gets for praying, he thinks—some monologue about this guy's grandfather, instead of the answer to understanding the dysfunctional relationship Billy has with his own father. Then suddenly he is struck by an epiphany, something that had never before occurred to him.

If you want to understand your own father," the voice deep within him says, "you must understand his father."

Billy thinks about this. He has always known the hard truth about his grandfather and the alcoholism that held a grip on him, as well as how little time his grandfather was around while his dad was growing up. But in this moment, a new light is shed over Billy's heart. And a love he has never felt for his own father now rises to the surface, filling him with the passionate, youthful freedom that had been stolen from him at such an early age.

In awe, he realizes that he has followed the instructions of that still, small voice within, and the very first man he asked to help gave him the answer to understanding his relationship with his father. And it had happened in a way he never could have imagined. Filled with a deep gratitude, Billy moves on to the ninth hole.

PASSION

THE NINTH HOLE

I will give them an undivided heart
and put a new spirit in them.
—Ezekiel 11:19

Bruce has the honors and tees his ball up first to hit his drive on number nine. He stands behind his ball and appears to Billy to be visualizing his tee shot. But before Bruce moves into his stance, he says, "This hole reminds me of how we have many different options in life. And how our success boils down to the choices we make."

Billy is no different from most men. He has made some very bad choices. He has lost everything in business with speculative ventures. His best decision was marrying his wife, but even his good decisions tend to turn out bitter in the end, as his commitment slowly fades. Even in his marriage this has happened. He has frequently even traveled to Scotland and other destinations, leaving his young family behind. He often justifies his decisions, even when they are destructive.

One of Billy's greatest issues is his lack of purpose. Without any definite purpose to guide his actions and decisions, Billy says yes to way too many things that come his way, while saying no to the very things in which he should be saying yes. This leaves Billy exhausted and drained of passion.

There was a passion that was unrequited in Billy's youth that he did not need to call upon to keep himself going on the golf course. It was just there, fresh with every shot. It is that passion that unmistakably shows in Billy's eyes as he makes the climb up to the ninth tee box. It can be difficult to adjust coming down from a mountaintop experience, but the ninth at Prairie Dunes is one amazing descent that continues the momentum in the golfer's experience.

Within Billy, there is a yearning undefined. Something different, more than just the fresh exhilaration of a golfing experience, is taking shape within Billy. This spiritual experience has ignited Billy's heart, and he is ready for something more.

The ninth hole faces back to the east, bringing the wide birth of native grass that bordered number eight into play once again to Billy's right, with more of the same flanking the left side of the fairway. The tee shot here is like stepping off a cliff, and what awaits is a crumpled fairway that looks like a carpet pushed up into giant folds. The shadows that move across this closely cropped turf in the early evening reveal a landscape alive, echoing the character and mystery found in places like St. Andrews or North Berwick. These places, while ancient in golfing, will forever bring out the youth in those who know them best.

Prairie Dunes is having an especially profound effect on Billy. The noticeable limp and chopping motion in his swing have now given way, and he is playing golf with a youthful passion. The ninth hole reveals this change from the start as his tee shot sails right into the tall grass, but Billy just smiles and puts another ball in play.

His approach to the green lands left of the green, and he stops to admire the movement of the landscape before pondering his next shot, because it could be played any number of ways. It could be putted, chipped, bumped or lobbed, and Billy seems rather amused by his options before bumping and running his ball up the steep slope to ten feet left of the hole, which rests in the highest part of this rolling green. This leaves Billy with a sharp left-to-right breaking putt that slides by the hole another five feet.

He misses that putt, but none of this seems to bother him, as he is passionately rapt in his own golfing adventure. He is not only once again playing the game he loves like he did when he was young; he is that boy again. He is yearning to live again. He is yearning to come alive as never before.

The Second Nine—The Battle Begins

COURAGE AND FOCUS

THE TENTH HOLE

*If anyone thinks he is something when he
is nothing, he deceives himself.*
—Galatians 6:3

It is only a matter of time before Prairie Dunes will test a golfer and tempt him back into the place from which he just escaped. And the tenth hole usually offers the perfect trap for the golfer. It is on the tenth hole where many golfers reset their expectations and, in the psyche, start a new round. Let a new battle begin afresh with hope of a new challenge to conquer.

Golf in this pure form can validate the question serving as more than just a metaphor as to whether the golfer has what it takes in battle. Here, winning may mean mustering the will just to enter into the fight. This, however, is not a fight against the golf course, but a battle with himself, a conflict that ultimately will test every man.

In truth, all Billy has to do is yield to the golf course and trust what is not only before him, but what he feels in his heart to be true. Prairie Dunes' tenth hole is deceptive, with a green as well as bunkers hidden and an elevation that is subtle, but profound. What on the surface looks like a simple hole can befuddle the golfer. But that is okay. After all, as in life, if golf was easy or even you might say fair or predictable, boredom would soon take hold. The true golfer needs a battle, but just like war, golf is not fair.

Bruce looks toward the hole and says, "Yes sir, this is where faith comes in. And it is an exciting adventure to embrace when you experience what you can't see as if it were certainly true. When you can't see an elevated green that is hidden, it makes it all the more exciting to find your ball resting next to the hole when arriving to the green." In saying this, Bruce understands this battle is one that must be faced with courage and not fear. He has learned that to find success, you must have absolute trust and abandon yourself to believe that even though you can't see the future in your heart, the certainty of what is going to happen is as real as if it has already taken place.

How do you do that? You let go and trust—give control to—another, instead of relying on yourself. To do that is a very frightening thing for most, but it is the key to overcoming fear.

This is a difficult proposition for Billy, who deep in his heart thinks all of his success is up to him. When Billy steps to the tenth tee to hit his ball, he feels that ever-familiar feeling of anxiety, which robs him of the freedom he has been experiencing.

Billy's tee shot at the tenth lands short of the green. He is fortunate to avoid the bunker to the right, but he still leaves himself a tricky chip shot that must flirt with the corner of the bunker if he is to go for the pin. He stubs his wedge in the ground during this attempt, and the ball squirts only a couple of feet, not even reaching the green.

He then stubs another pitch. His ball listlessly scoots onto the green, and after three putts he finally finishes the hole.

Billy is not sure whether his misfortune on the tenth hole is due to a lack of concentration or too much relaxation. On the outside, none of this seems to faze him as he moves on to the eleventh hole, but his recent enjoyment has now once again turned into an all-too-familiar despair. He trudges off into the wilderness to face himself again.

INTO THE WILDERNESS

THE ELEVENTH HOLE

But God showed his great love for us by sending
Christ to die for us while we were still sinners.
—Romans 5:8

When the deepest places of the heart have been ignored and then swept clean, freedom can turn to despair, or worse, resignation. For when you received a glimpse and even heard the voice of God, what great expectation awaits you? Then, when you find yourself alone again and feeling that familiar pain, it can create doubt.

"Was it real?" Billy whispers to himself.

Perhaps it's just all in his mind, he thinks— that voice he heard and all the memories swirling around in his head. This yearning inside him is so emotional. Billy wonders if he's having a midlife crisis? After all, with everything Billy has done, he wonders how anyone—especially

God—would choose to care about him? How could anyone really love him?

Billy thinks back to when he found out he was adopted and how, in that moment, he realized his entire life was a lie—and he made a subconscious agreement that at all costs, he would protect himself from that type of pain. He would make himself an island, building a wall that nobody could pass through.

What Billy does not know is the truth of his adoption and how his birth mother had decided, in spite of the option to abort her pregnancy, that because of Jesus Christ, she would carry Billy until birth. Billy also doesn't know that his mother, the wonderful woman who loved him, chose to adopt him even though she had become pregnant during the adoption process. These details and so much more of how God has orchestrated and delivered Billy to this very day are hidden from him.

Furthermore, Billy is blind to the fact that his self-preserving wall of protection—which keeps him in the delusion of believing he is the only person he can truly rely on—has led to so much of the despair and isolation he is feeling at this very moment.

With these wilderness memories beginning to swirl around in his head, Billy steps up to the eleventh tee.

The eleventh hole brushes by the only body of water on Prairie Dunes, a pond to the left just beyond the tee box that, barring a horrid tee shot, does not come into play. To the left, out of bounds, is dense wilderness of impenetrable tall grass. From the tee, this two-shot hole appears to be rather benign from tee to green. The fairway draws to the left on a level plain until it reaches the green where a large hummock fronts the green, deflecting any direct attempt away from the putting surface.

The smart play is a running shot just left of this obstacle, which must skirt by a large bunker to the right. The hole is perfectly positioned to lull the golfer into a false sense of security. While not appearing as difficult at first glance, the hole is an unexpected challenge. Just the slightly pulled ball will be lost in the tall grass to the left. And while the safer play is to the right, this shot also means a longer and more difficult approach will await.

The feeling of emptiness and weariness Billy feels on the tee continues to deepen. The desire for the thrill or presence of the high Billy found playing the previous holes is overshadowing the eleventh hole. In reality, this hole provides the possibility to peacefully reflect on the greatness just experienced, all while staying in the moment. Unfortunately, this lull in the round can also lead to a loss of heart.

Billy finally seems to steady himself enough to move ahead, and he hits a tee shot that perfectly positions him for success. As Billy makes his way to his ball, his thoughts drift again to Megan, a memory that has very much shaped him, though he would like to forget it. This memory is key to the man he has become, for it is not just his adoption story, but a series of blows, that has led him to isolate and lose the trust in others. Earlier in the round, Billy was successful at keeping this memory from coming to the surface, but now he cannot force the recollections down. The thoughts that flood from the depths of his heart are as fresh and painful as if they happened only yesterday.

Megan was Billy's first love. They had met at a church event when he was a teenager, and he fell hard for her. They spent hours upon hours talking on the phone, and in each moment when they were not together, his thoughts would drift to her. She was his first real obsession. He trusted Megan above all people, and he believed she truly cared about him for who he was. But that, too, was a lie.

Ironically for Billy, the betrayal he experienced happened at summer church camp. To make it all the more painful and damaging, his betrayal came at the hand of his best friend, who revealed the hard truth by cheating on him with Megan during camp. This event devastated Billy, and this and other blows like it would help create the man he was today. And what is more, he had become the very type of person he despised.

With this fresh memory and the regret of who he has become burning inside him, he loses his second shot to the right, where it hangs up in the thick grass in front of the right bunker. He then hits his next shot over the green, feebly chipping his next shot onto the green, before three-putting to finish the hole off.

Billy moves on to the dramatically elevated twelfth tee box perched high upon the dune, where for Billy his fight for freedom continues. All the while, he barely notices that Bruce is faithfully and compassionately continuing along with him on his journey as they climb the stairs together.

A CHILD OF GOD

THE TWELFTH HOLE

*Blessed are the poor in spirit, for theirs
is the kingdom of heaven.*
—Matthew 5:3

As Billy and Bruce make it to the top of the tall dune, Bruce looks into the valley below and says, "We don't need to do much here, other that trust the wind and allow it to help us on our way." Wise words—yet Billy is so engrossed in his own personal struggles that he doesn't even notice Bruce's comment.

When Billy started out on his journey as a man, he was full of pride. Until today, deep down all that was left in him was an empty sadness. Now deep down, Billy knows there is something more, but he doesn't know exactly what it is, or if he'll ever find it. Due to his wounds, Billy has viewed the world and his actions as neither good nor bad, believing he existed in a very complicated gray area. Now, Billy can see the truth of his emptiness inside, and it is mingled with a hope that his new heart is about to be filled.

What will Billy find in this awakening? This realization that what he had become in his life was not just the way he was, but instead the result of being a broken man in a shattered world. He never before believed he could change. And for many years, the diversions and pleasures of this world were enough to give Billy some satisfaction, helping to get him through each long, lonely, tiring day. But as the years wore on, his lack of true purpose left him hungry for something more.

Ironically, the very weakness that Billy is trying to escape holds the key to finding a strength he never imagined could be his. And he is very much feeling this weakness as he arrives at the twelfth hole.

The twelfth tee looks down onto the low-lying northernmost corner of Prairie Dunes. Here for the first time, trees come into play. Two large cottonwoods stand guard on either side of the fairway. They do not impact the tee shot, but if the golfer's drive is too close to them, they will alter the second shot into one of the trickiest greens on the course. There is a lone fairway bunker to the left and thick vegetation beyond it. To the right there is more room to miss, and this is where Billy pushes his drive.

He creatively chokes down on an iron and plays between the trees, but the shot drifts to the right and rolls off the back of the green. He then attempts to chip onto the green, and while his ball successfully finds the green, it only does so by a few feet. Rattled, he follows that up by blowing his first putt fifteen feet past the cup. His next attempt appears to stop five feet past the hole, only to catch a slope and slide another five feet farther from the hole.

He goes on to miss his next putt and then misses a three-footer before finally dropping his ball into the cup.

Billy's fire has dimmed. He does not feel angry or even upset about the woes of his roller coaster golf game. He has accepted his fate, resigned to the fact that none of this matters, and he can't do anything about his misfortune anyway. At the moment, he feels very much alone. The clouds have darkened over the dunes and in his heart.

As Billy heads to the thirteenth tee, he feels neither hot nor cold. And as a golfer knows, this is the state of mind where the course is sure to spit out what is left of your game. It is here in this state, without expectation and dying to self, that Billy may find his way beyond the brokenness and pain, into freedom from the whims of this world. Perfect freedom, perfect peace, and finally the purpose to go on living could be closer than Billy will ever know. He realizes he can no longer live life alone, without purpose, in his own strength. He needs a friend and mentor to help show him the way.

Holes 13, 14 and 15—Learning how to Fight

FINDING STRENGTH IN ANOTHER

THE THIRTEENTH HOLE

As iron sharpens iron, so one person sharpens another.
—Proverbs 27:17

When you are in a battle, being alone is dangerous. Nobody has your back, and you are isolated in your thoughts and vulnerable to being taken out by the enemy. (And be assured, we do have an enemy.) Solitude is important, but to make progress with any endeavor, eventually you are going to need help. You will need someone to join you on your journey, someone who can help show you the way. A warrior is not born in and of himself; he needs training.

Billy needs a mentor and a friend.

The thirteenth hole plays back into the teeth of the wind that now roars between the dunes in a ferocity that will bring a golfer to his knees. This is not the situation for anything less than determination, focus and guts, but

Billy swings with a less than committed swing, and the ball is caught straight up into the torrential wind. Like a boomerang, it flies to the right and then back toward him. The ball lands at the feet of Bruce. He picks up the ball, looks at Billy with a compassionate, sympathetic smile and hands it to him, saying, "You're having quite the adventure today."

Up to this point, Billy has been playing very much alone and isolated in his own thoughts. Now, however, Billy begins to open up and to truly start playing golf together with Bruce.

Bruce pulls one of his hickory-shafted driving irons from his vintage canvas golf bag. Until now, Billy hasn't even noticed Bruce's unusual choice in golf clubs. Bruce drops a ball in front of him, takes a look down the fairway, and without so much as a waggle he takes the club straight back over his shoulder. Effortlessly, he brings it back down until it lightly rests on his left shoulder. The resulting reaction is a ball boring through the wind, low and straight, landing just at the point the thirteenth makes its turn to the left, revealing the elevated green in the distance.

Billy tees up his ball again and swings furiously, making a sound strike. But this time, the ball sharply turns to the left and disappears into a grassy dune. His next drive finds the fairway, but far behind Bruce's ball.

As the two men make their way down the fairway, Bruce starts up the conversation. "Yes, indeed, you sure are having quite a serious adventure today."

"I guess you could call it that," Billy retorts, shaking his from side to side.

"Yes, this course sets one up for quite an adventure," Bruce continues as they make their way up the fairway. They reach Bruce's ball, where he once again wastes no time in addressing his game with the same silkiness as before. He sends his ball piercing through the wind. It softly lands on the green, coming to rest just a few feet from the hole.

Billy has scrambled all the way to the thirteenth green. Now as a spectator lost in admiration, he watches Bruce tap in for his birdie.

In the moment, Billy seems no longer to be concerned with his golf game, as he seems more enamored with understanding Bruce. There is something different about Bruce, even beyond his unquenchable zest for life, that inspires Billy. It is this very companionship that infuses a new vigor into his step as he makes his way to the fourteenth hole.

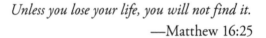

THE POINT OF IT ALL

THE FOURTEENTH HOLE

Unless you lose your life, you will not find it.
—Matthew 16:25

Bruce smiles and says, "Too bad most golfers don't understand even a great golf course like this one means nothing, but it has the potential to help them find everything. For some, the golf course is exactly where they need to be, but for others it can be the worst place in the world to tarry. Take me, for example. I lost everything in the name of golf. My wife, my children—"

He pauses, his voice cracking, then goes on.

"—My world came crashing down around me, but the golf course was the one place where I thought I could find my escape. But, Bill, the links became my prison. Keeping me from real life!"

Bruce and Billy were now standing on the fourteenth tee, with Billy listening intently to his fellow golfer's story.

68

"You see, the way I used to play a hole like this one was to try to bite off as much as I could chew. Taking as much risk on the golf course as possible was, for me, a way to feel alive."

And indeed, the fourteenth hole at Prairie Dunes is from the tee a par 4 of the risk-reward variety. Perhaps the most sharply bending par 4 on the course, the fourteenth hole's fairway wraps around a huge, nasty, sandy waste area to the left before turning at a nearly ninety-degree angle and making its way to the green, which sits low slung at the base of a grove of huge cottonwood trees.

Both of our golfers hit fine drives. Bruce takes a safer route to the right, which easily carries the hazard. Billy makes a riskier play at it and barely makes it across, but his ball trickles onto the fairway, leaving him closer to the green in excellent position. On the way to hit their next shots, Bruce continues the conversation.

"Bill, I perceive you to be a Christian. I perceived myself to be one once, but in reality I was anything but a Christian. On the outside I was a nice guy, trying to do everything the right way, run my business, control what others thought of me. What they saw, I tried to make as impressive as possible. But really, I was so filled with fear and anger. My golf game made matters worse."

"I know the feeling," said Billy with a chuckle.

"Yes, Bill, but unlike you it was the success of my golf game that kept me troubled," said Bruce with a smile. "You see, I did not take up this noble game until I was forty, but from the moment I picked up a club, I was hooked. In a very short time after obsessive-compulsive practice,

I was what you might call a scratch golfer. I had one goal in my life—improving my score. Some might call what I did a dream come true, but I was in the middle of my own self-absorbed nightmare. In reality, I was on the run, worn out and on the verge, even though I did not see it then, of complete self-destruction. Which, as it turns out, is exactly what I needed."

Billy finds himself thinking of his own life, of his wife and his children. They are slipping through his hands, he suddenly realizes. He thinks back to the times he has abandoned them and how he has blamed his wife for holding him back and has resented her for times she has vented her frustration over his flirtations with golf and his other vices.

At this point, Billy and Bruce arrive at their tee shots. Bruce softly strokes his second onto the green, but Billy pulls his second shot into the bunker guarding the left side of the green.

"That's not going to be good," says Bruce, while taking a ball out of his pocket and dropping it in front of Billy. "Why don't you go ahead and hit another one?" Billy agrees to this, knocking his next shot up just short of the green.

"What happened? How did you find your way?" asks Billy, rapt by what he is hearing.

"It was this little slice of heaven that did it." Bruce turns to gaze back over the land they have just traversed, like a delighted parent might look at his own child.

"On a day very much like today, I had one of the most incredible experiences. While I was walking this very course, I felt God come alongside me, reassuring me, giving me His strength, opening my eyes to what really matters, offering His presence as only the true Father can. And in that moment, this golf course became the most beautiful place I had ever seen."

Bruce now paused, then turned to make eye contact with Billy. "That day, God revealed the truth that had somehow escaped me all these years. You know how Jesus said, 'I am the way, the truth and the life'?"

Billy nods.

"I learned that day that meaning can come only from God. Not work, golf or even family. It is God who provides joy and everything that matters. That day, for the first time, I stopped focusing on myself and started walking with God. In essence, my life began that day."

Bruce leans in toward Billy, as if sharing a secret. "There is an extra measure of joy in the golf game of one who has not been visiting the course to take care of the ones he loves. When a golfer tends first to what matters most and meets the challenges of the world head on, they live with a steely resolve that brings out the best in their golf game. No golf lessons, practice, or personal discipline can bring out the depth and power that comes from brokenness—for from this pain, freedom is found in the game. And more importantly, the person is never the same.

"Bill, if you have ever fasted, you will understand that the same thing that happens to your body during self-denial and hunger, this golf course offers to the golfer. It truly drains you, removing every expectation, until at last you are free. And this golf course, much in the same way as fasting, purifies and leaves you open for more depth of understanding of your golf game, your life, and even your relationship with God. It is God using, like He does with food in a fast, the very thing that gives us enjoyment and fulfillment to lovingly break us, thus releasing the ability to take our experience with him to another level. But it isn't easy. And let's face it—today, most people want the easy way in everything they do. But it just does not work that way with God."

This whole conversation has taken place right before Billy is about to hit his next shot. Now, he realizes afresh that it is his turn to take another swing. Pondering the words he has just heard, he studies his ball, which is in a seriously bad downhill lie, sunny side up in the sand with ten yards of carry to the green which is severely sloping away from him.

He steps away from the second ball he had stroked close to the green and says, "I think I'll hit my first ball."

To place his ball anywhere close to the hole from this position will take a miracle, and that is just what Billy produces. He makes a low trajectory, driving shot that just clears the lip of the bunker. With amazing back spin, the ball skids, hits the flagstick, and settles just inches from the hole. Billy raises his arms above his head in victory.

Bruce smiles. "Now, that is how it's done!"

"If I would have hit that second ball, I would never have just experienced the thrill of that last shot," says Billy.

And Bruce adds, "You also would not have the freedom you now possess."

LOSING SELF-CONSCIOUSNESS

THE FIFTEENTH HOLE

> *"Look! I stand at the door and knock. If you hear my voice and open the door, I will come in, and we will share a meal together as friends."*
> —Revelation 3:20

The conversation continues as Bruce and Billy head to the fifteenth hole, the longest par 3 on the course. It requires a long iron or even a wood to reach the putting surface. And it's named "The Shoot" because you must thread your ball carefully between two giant cottonwood trees onto the elevated green.

"What do you mean by freedom?" Billy asks Bruce.

"I mean freedom from being self-conscious, or only playing your game. Letting go of our habitual, self-obsessed, competitive expectation and not fighting for what we want. This does not mean leaving expectation behind, but instead living full of positive expectation, regardless of the outcome of the shot we just hit."

Bruce points to the green they are aiming for. "Take this hole, for example. We have a pre-shot routine and visualization of what we hope to happen, but what happens to most golfers if disaster strikes? We are no longer able to stay in the moment, and we become a prisoner to that which was meant to help us succeed."

Billy ponders this quietly.

"Do you mind if I ask you a more personal question?" Bruce asks.

"Sure."

"How did you feel when I let you know my perception of you was that of a Christian?"

"Well, it just isn't something you expect to talk about on the golf course," says Billy.

"It made you uncomfortable, didn't it?" replies Bruce. Billy nods in agreement, but Bruce puts him at ease with his next words. "Don't feel embarrassed about it, Billy. Talking of God makes most men quite uneasy."

Bruce and Billy both hit perfect shots through the shoot, their golf balls landing softly on the green beyond. Bruce once again dives back into the conversation.

"That was a nice swing."

"Yes indeed, there was definitely freedom in that golf shot," Billy agrees.

"You know, our relationship with Jesus is an awful lot like a golfer's newfound freedom," Bruce shares. "Jesus comes knocking at the door of our hearts and He keeps it up until one day, when we have run out of all the answers on our little, frustrating course in life, we welcome Him in. Then Jesus makes our life like a Prairie Dunes to live."

Bruce gestures toward the beautiful landscape that surrounds them. "Wild, free and full of adventure, not the way most perceive their lives to become when they become a Christian. Many feel they are giving up their lives, when the truth is, God is stepping into their lives to give them the answers to the questions that have so long been elusive to them. To understand what it really means to be a man, and that there is a purpose God has for their lives."

Purpose! Billy's eyes light up as he considers the possibility. How long has he struggled with feeling a sense of purpose? Bruce notices this realization Billy is having, and he nods and continues his sharing.

"Many men think that after all they have done and who they've become, there is no way that God could ever care, or have something meant for them to do. Most men have wounds that have been inflicted on them by the very people who were supposed to love them. The perceptions of what reality is has been skewed by these wounds. For a man, the greatest wound is usually given to him by his father."

Father. It's a powerful word.

Billy thinks of his own father, and the struggles he experienced growing up, wanting to please his own father and prove himself. He is like so many of the men who have walked my hills at Prairie Dunes, looking for success when what they truly crave is love.

Many fathers dedicate themselves to helping their children succeed in a sport like golf, and who can argue with a few of the results? It could be said these children are blessed to have a father who is always there sacrificing so his child can succeed. But a young man needs much more than the presence, instruction, or tips that a father in this world can give. A boy certainly yearns to be blessed and affirmed, but only a relationship with his true Father, God, will lead him into what it means to be a man, so that the ultimate foundation in Christ is laid within the young man's heart. For Christ is the only one who will sustain him when his earthly father is gone.

Without this depth of divine love to draw upon, a boy will attempt to rely on his own strength to find his way in life. It is perhaps, I would imagine, like seeking that perfect round of golf. It is not going to happen. The way to find life, or to fill the void, is by walking—or in Billy's case, golfing—with his true Father.

Yes, hole by hole——walking with God.

THE POWER OF PURPOSE

THE SIXTEEN HOLE

*Jesus replied, "Very truly I tell you, no one can see
the kingdom of God unless they are born again."*
—John 3:3

With impeccable timing, the sun breaks through as Billy
and Bruce arrive at the sixteenth hole, casting a spotlight
on the prairie in all its splendor.

"Isn't this place amazing? It is truly alive," says Bruce.
"Do you know what makes this so especially stunning? It
is fire! You see, the folks that run Prairie Dunes understand
the truth that unless this land is cleansed, it will ultimately
never be what it was meant to be.

"God does the same with us, for if we do not die, we
cannot truly live. This is even more incredible when you
consider that God can take all our mistakes and sin—you
know, we were born with a few weeds, and without God

we can make quite a mess out of our own plot of land. But He can burn it all away, so that what remains is truly born again, and free to grow into all it was created to be."

Billy and Bruce hit perfect drives, with each of their balls coming to rest in the middle, but on this uphill hole into the wind, they each still face a lengthy approach shot to a pin well guarded by a bunker to the right. On the way to their next shot, Billy chimes in.

"Bruce, I understand what you mean by born again, but why after we are born again, do we have to keep getting burned over and over?"

"Well, Bill, you know we have a cunning enemy. And just like the weeds that will keep finding their way into the prairie without fire to burn them away, so does sin keep cropping up in our lives to tempt us. We live in a fallen world. As the weeds lie in wait on this golf course, we have an enemy in Satan who does the same, trying his best to turn poor choices into a plot full of sin and shame. If we allow him to run wild, just like the weeds, he'll ruin our lives.

"And so God, as a loving Father, repeatedly offers His cleansing grace, as often as we need it. Hopefully, over time, our relationship with Him becomes like playing Prairie Dunes—full of exciting, amazing adventure, with less and less frustration over the inevitable mistakes we will make.

"Unfortunately, Billy, the only flames many men will ever experience will come upon them too late, bringing horrible destruction. Let's say, for instance, a golfer comes to a desert course. Through his round, he has his ups and downs, but he keeps on trying, keeps on going, giving it his best, and he has just enough success to keep on playing, pressing on, feeling the occasional adrenaline that comes from that perfect shot. Along the way, in this round that is most memorable, he receives good results even when his execution does not merit it. So he arrives at the conclusion of his round and finds himself facing the approach to the eighteenth green. He says to himself, 'Come on now, you have to finish strong,' which is the very thing the world has always told him.

"Only now, the pressure has begun to build, and his self-willed energy is waning. To make matters worse, the eighteenth green is fronted by water and there is sand behind it. So, he chunks his next shot. Then, his next attempt sails over the green and into the bunker, leaving him a down-lie. And after three futile attempts, his fourth shot crosses over the green and into the water. Now our golfer has gone from determined to resigned to his fate. You see, this golfer only had one ball left, in what turns out to be his final round, so not only can he not finish strong—he can't finish at all. The fire of rage and bitterness consumes him.

"This is the picture of most men's lives, but this does not have to be this way for you and me. With God, we can rest in His presence, and He will be our strength. When we hit into the water, He will give us as many balls and into eternity as many holes as we find joy in playing the game hole by hole with Him.

"And Billy, trust me—God wants to kindle a fire in you, and when the flames begin to burn, golf and life will never be the same."

Our two golfers' approaches miss the sixteenth green, with Billy landing short of the bunker and Bruce flying his shot over the putting surface, leaving both golfers with tricky third shots. Billy's approach once again almost goes in the hole. Bruce follows Billy by nearly knocking his next shot in the hole. They both slip away to the seventeenth with pars and plenty of momentum.

THE CLEAR VIEW OF FREEDOM IS STRAIGHT BEFORE YOU

THE SEVENTEENTH HOLE

*No one else should carry the title of "Father"; you
have only one Father, and he's in heaven.*
                                        —Matthew 23:9

The seventeenth hole at Prairie Dunes is no mystery. Straight before the golfer lies the green perched in the distance. This par 5 is simple, straightforward, but it is not easy. There are no bunkers, and the fairway sits on a level plain that awaits Billy and Bruce as they arrive at the tee.

Billy's confidence has given way to joy in the present. Confusion and pain stunted by self-awareness—really, self-pity—is now replaced by fluid movement, effortless in every way. Swinging without thought, striding with power, eyes fixed and on fire, Billy feels every bit the energetic youth that once made the golfing fairways his playground.

Now, however, a sense of purpose streams from him that has nothing to do with golf and everything to do with really living. He has found what he has been looking for—a reality that, in and of itself, he would have avoided at all costs if he had not met God on the golf course. Billy's old, hard heart has been utterly, painfully ripped from him, and the procedure has been lovingly performed with the surgical precision that only God can offer. Now, a new heart beats in him, and where so much youth was wasted, now a deep purpose abides within him.

In him, the promise that God will restore the years is fulfilled.

Standing in the seventeenth fairway as they prepare to hit their third shot, Bruce and Billy continue to converse like lifelong friends or brothers.

"Do you know what golf is to most men?" Bruce asks Billy. "It is another bandage to hide their wounds. It's an attempt to warm their cold hearts. Hearts as frigid as the wind when this day began for you. This game is to them just another one of many selfish idols that only lead to destruction.

"So many are fulfilling what the Scriptures say about men having a form of glory, but all of it is just in and of themselves. They are much like—"

Billy interrupts to confess, "Like I used to be. My life was constructed around me, and I couldn't even see it. The truth is that God has been working on me for a while before bringing me here today. I mistook arrogance for self-confidence, and that gave way to self-pity when things did not please me the way I thought they should.

"I traded my deepest desires for shame and proceeded to lose everything, including all of my relationships and possessions, until all that remained was pain and regret. Once I was emptied, God began to fill me. He gave me a beautiful wife and child, providing everything I could have hoped for, but my guilt, shame and striving continued until today."

Billy looks around the course, pondering the experience he has had on the course. Then he turns back to Bruce, continuing to explain his thoughts.

"When I arrived here, feeling cold and in pain, dealing with so much uncertainty away from the course... Bruce, I had found myself going through the motions, not really trusting that things would get better. Still not letting go of my striving and manipulating ways. But today, hole by hole, God has shown me that if I walk His course, He will fill me with His fire for life!"

Bruce smiles. "Yes, Billy, we have all been dead while experiencing our brief time in this fleshly existence. But all it takes is a spark to kindle our dry and withering hearts, just as you found out today. But my hope for you is that you always remember the freedom you feel right now and what it means to walk hole by hole with God."

The two golfers turn to study the course ahead of them.

Fear is what the third shot on hole 17 generates in most golfers, as this approach is perhaps the most harrowing on the entire golf course. The severely rolling green sits high on a hillside, perched above the fairway with steep drop-offs to either side. To the right, a wayward shot finds deep rough without hope of seeing the putting surface from that lie. To the left, a bunker lies at the bottom of the abyss. The simple first two shots seem to lull most golfers to sleep, and they meet a gruesome end when they reach the green.

Making the matter even more difficult for Billy and Bruce is the fact that today the pin placement is just a few paces from a steep roll back into the fairway below or into the bunker, making a direct assault a bold one indeed.

First up is Bruce, and he fires a low, stinging wedge that skips to the right of the flag and comes to rest in the middle of the green. Next, Billy steps over the ball and confidently strikes a lofted shot that lands just inches to the left of the hole and stops just shy of the bunker, leaving a ten-foot birdie putt that he rolls in the cup. Bruce two-putts for his par.

It is off to the eighteenth hole they go, with Billy looking like a completely different man.

SETTING A NEW COURSE

THE EIGHTEENTH HOLE

> Then he said to his disciples, "The Harvest is plentiful
> but the workers are few. Ask the Lord of the harvest,
> therefore, to send out workers into his harvest field."
>
> — Matthew 9:37-38

As Billy and Bruce make their way to the eighteenth hole,
Bruce tells Billy that before him many challenges, trials and
tests now will face him as he walks with God.

"Remember," Bruce says to Billy, "regardless of what
gifts God gives you through your relationship with Him,
it will be His love in your life that matters most, for that is
what people will see in you that will truly show that God
is real."

As Bruce finishes this statement, they both arrive at
the eighteenth tee box perched above the final, crisp green
fairway of the day. The entire scene before them is made

all the more vivid in the waning sunlight. The golfers take in one last view of the dunes and the flowing prairie grass.

The par-4 final hole doesn't require a long drive off the tee, but the shot does need to be precise. An easy swing should do it and each golfer swings easily, but Billy's golf ball finds its way out to the right onto a massive dune that follows the hole to the green. Bruce joins Billy as he makes his way to the area where Billy's ball has landed, and they find it on the steeply sloping dune in the deep grass. They both look at the green in the distance.

Bruce smiles and says, "This sure is a great example of a trial and a test. A mentor of mine once explained to me what you are facing right now in golfing terms. Billy, God has a plan for you, and it is called par. You stood on the tee and picked the right club, tested the wind, adjusted your stance, and gave a smooth, sweet swing. You sought to place your ball into the fairway, and you did everything right. And yet your ball has come to rest here in the rough.

"When we look up from here, we still see the flag in the same place. God's will has not moved. Your desire for par remains, and yet your ball is in this deep grass. You could throw your club, storm off the course, and be like Job's wife said, 'Curse God and die.' I've watched many men, including my own father, do just that many times. I have done that myself before—just given up before embracing God's Grace.

"Instead, Billy, regardless of what happens, you must choose to play out the hole. Par is now more difficult, but it's still your goal. I refuse to credit God for the slice or the hook, and I give Him glory for the ability to play the game.

God is good all the time."

Billy replies, "Bruce, that is a good way to look at things, but I have to tell you that I'm really tired of God always being in the distance."

"Billy," Bruce says, "God isn't far away from you. He is right before you (Psalm 16:8-11 NKJV). He lives in you and walks with you."

Bruce continues, "It is His will that is ever before you, and as you remain in Christ, you will find yourself ever more freely wrapped in God's Grace. For you were saved by Grace—for yet when we were still sinners, Christ died for us—and it is a free gift given to you in Him."

Billy smiles, hitting his next shot back into the fairway. And he is back on track on his way to finishing a round he will never forget.

Bruce and Billy finish the hole. The two golfers remove their hats and shake hands. Then something unexpected happens. Bruce looks Billy in the eye, then places his hand on Billy's shoulder. Bruce bows his head, and he begins to pray aloud in a bold, deep voice.

"Father, thank You for bringing us together today. For orchestrating and doing what we could never do ourselves. For loving us with such an amazing love filled with such grace. I thank You for Billy. For the man You have called him to be. That he will grow to know You and to live for You, that he may continue to experience the incredible freedom that is only available through Your Son, Jesus. Be with him as he leaves here today. Protect him on his journey home. Bless his marriage and his children, helping him lead them as only You can do. I pray this in the name of my Savior and King, Jesus Christ. Amen."

Billy and Bruce both look up to see a young man standing there. He is in his late twenties or early thirties, and he is smiling from ear to ear, and he says, "That was awesome! What do you guys do?"

Bruce looks at the young man and says, "We're brothers in Christ!"

The man introduces himself, "I'm Ethan, and I've just started to know God and read the Bible. There is so much more to the Bible than I ever imagined."

Billy says, "God bless you, Ethan. Would you mind if I prayed for you today?" Ethan gladly accepts, and Billy begins to pray for the young man. As Billy is praying, joy fills him, for he has realized for the first time he has been part of a moment that has eternally influenced someone else. And now Billy wants more!

Billy turns to share his excitement with Bruce, but he is gone. Vanished! Billy looks down and resting on his golf bag he sees a fresh Prairie Dunes scorecard alongside the pieces of the old scorecard Billy had disposed of earlier in his round. Billy picks up the pieces, surprised to see them. Then he notices that there is a note written on the brand-new, blank scorecard. It reads:

"Billy, always remember to remain in Him. 'I am the vine; you are the branches. If you remain in Me and I in you, you will bear much fruit; apart from Me you can do nothing' (John 15:5). As Jesus says here, you can do nothing without Him. And with Him all things are possible, including putting back together all the pieces in your round of golf today and giving you a new life."

As Billy walks off the eighteenth green, he commits with resolve to loving his wife and leading his family as his first ministry. He thinks of how he has changed today, and before him lies his next ministry—to help another find his way back to God. To help other men remain with God moment by moment, day by day, hole by hole, finding true life on the course they were meant to play.

This transformation can be yours as well, dear reader. The freedom you once had as a child can be found again, just like Billy on this blustery day. You, too, can walk with God moment by moment, finding your true life, and your full purpose, playing the course He has set before you with joy. That is my prayer for you—now and always.

Contact the Author

holebyhole@gmail.com